Texas... to Get Horses

Collected Poems

Kimberly G. Wieser

Introduction by Juanita Pahdopony

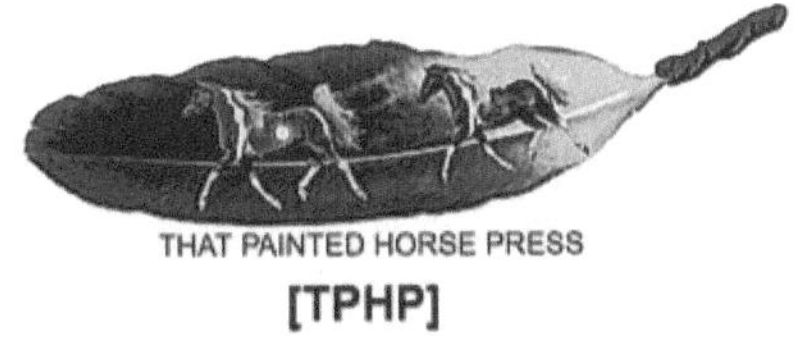

Harrah, Oklahoma
Calgary, Alberta
2019

Native Writers' Circle of the Americas

That Painted Horse Press: A Borderless Indigenous Press of the Americas

WWW.THATPAINTEDHORSEPRESS.ORG

Acknowledgements

"Right Fist Up." Upcoming in *The Beatest State in the Union: An Anthology of Beat Texas Writers*. Eds. Chris Carmona, Rob Johnson, and Chuck Taylor. Austin: U of Texas P.

"kitchen table refuge." *Women Write Resistance: Poets Resist Gender Violence.* Ed. Laura Madeline Wiseman. Pittsburg: Hyacinth Girl Press, 2013: 157; *Sentence* 7 (2009): 143.

"U-ne-ga." Kuikatl 30 Mar. 2012.

"Na he dum" and "Sweet Brown Honey." *Black Magnolias: A Literary Journal* 4.4 (2011): 41–43.

"Courtship," and "Long Woman." *Yellow Medicine Review* (Fall 2011): 62–69.

"A Song to Tell Robert Bly How We Do This in My Language," "Texas Traces," and "U-ne-ga." *The People Who Stayed Behind: Southeastern Indian Writing After the Removal.* Eds. Geary Hobson and Janet McAdams. Norman: U of Oklahoma P, 2010: 309–16.

"Diaspora." Poem. CCTE *Studies* 68 (2003): 60-62.

"Carnival Pictures." *Frontiers: A Journal of Women's Studies* 23.2 (2002): 92–93.

"The Real Americana." *This Bridge We Call Home: Radical Visions for Transformation.* Eds. Gloria E. Anzaldúa and AnaLouise Keating. New York: Routledge, 2002. 155–58.

"Maid in America" is from "Selections from Breeds and Outlaws." *Children of the Dragonfly.* Ed. Robert Bensen. Tucson: U of Arizona P, 2001. 191–95.

"A Song to Tell Robert Bly How We Do This in My Language." *Studies in American Indian Literatures* 12.3 (2000): 84.

Dedication

For Rance
because I'm so blessed to ride off
into the sunset with you.
U̶ra for taking my hand
and pulling me up onto your horse.

"She just closes her eyes and she holds on tight,
and she lets that pony run..."
from "Let That Pony Run," *Homeward Looking Angel,*
recorded by Pam Tillis, 1993

Map of Contents

Introduction

As both a writer and visual artist, powerful art openings, with exceptional art, often leave me over stimulated and feeling somewhat disordered. Perhaps it is sensory overload and my inability to process so much excellence in a single visit. Over the years, I've learned to focus on artists and patrons, quickly scanning the art that commands my attention. Another day, I would return to appreciate, absorb, and read artist iconographies without all the distractions. Kim Wieser's *Texas ... to Get Horses* is like viewing a colorful kaleidoscope of fine art. Her poetry takes the reader on an epic journey through early life of a "mixed blood" with its underlying issues of social, cultural, and economic factors that impact underrepresented minorities in our country. Early on, I scanned the body of poetry and randomly read from the back to the front. When I began to feel the familiar stages of sensory overload, I made a list of exactly how to read *Texas ... to Get Horses*:

I. Read the poems chronologically–it's a journey not a marathon.

II. Savor the poems with all your senses–don't be ashamed to cry.

III. Increase your knowledge base of issues in Indian Country.

IV. *Waltz Across Texas*–Hey, smell the sage, we reached home!

Southern plains Comanche have a long history of taking captives. And while there are explanations, no one can dispute the number of captives who decided they no longer wanted to return to their former lives and found a new Comanche home. After all, home is sanctuary. There were reasons Comanche took captives: a high incidence of infant mortality, considering the nomadic horse culture lifestyle for pregnant women. Another reason was the value of returned captives through ransom and trade. That said, Comanche captive history and its mixed blood history strengthened the Comanche bands through exposure to different foods, medicines, clothing, shelter, and spirituality, while building a richer knowledge base beyond the traditional knowledge of the band's leaders and their families.

Kimberly Wieser sees herself as a "Texas girl raised on stories of Cynthia Ann Parker" and as a woman of many heritages, who identifies with "mixed blood and mixed ways." Similarly, this also describes many American Indian people today. Today's Comanche are mixed blood, and while a few claim full blood status, their DNA ancestry might be surprising.

Wieser's title poem, a pantoum, conjures up painful images of the 1874 killing of over a thousand horses in Tule Canyon, in a Mackenzie campaign to put Comanche on foot, in the dead of winter. It was a horrifying solution to rid Texas of its last remaining American Indians. At once, the reader connects the dots of Comanche history of taking captives; the killing of the horses, and the strength and enigma of enduring love of a captive for her captor.

> "We went to Texas to get horses.
> Your women followed us home"
> Comanche men laugh, teasing the
> Mexicans.
> All the Nums had captive grandmas.

Identity, melancholia for the past, and home are three recurring themes throughout Wieser's writings. "Moon Cookie Summers" and "Kitchen Table Refuge" gives us a salty and sweet taste of life in Texas through our tears and laughter. Although impacted by alcoholism and a history of poverty, there is nevertheless a binding love of family. Those who grew up in similar ways, where communal lifeways meant resources were shared by family and extended family, will identify with these poems. Surely, our historic past lives as communal people existing within our sacred genetic memories. How does one explain those who describe themselves as "living richly" within the culture and in similar ways of their surrounding community, while others (generally outsiders) consider them, by their standards, as living in poverty?

"Sick of Being Haunted by Ana Mendieta" is my chosen powerful poem. Sadly, I associate it with the "missing and murdered Indigenous women," which is currently a common issue in Indian County and Indian social media. However, it is not addressed in national media because, as Rush Limbaugh said years ago about the Indian mascot issue, "Who cares what 2% of the population thinks?" Yet school mascots represent historic and institutional racism and perpetuate negative stereotypes. Caricatures of Indians disregard personhood and are hurtful to children. I read "Sick of being Haunted by Ana Mendieta" in the sanctuary and comfort of my home. However, when I became so affected by this poem, I put it away, went outdoors to calm my spirit and gather my strength because I was moved to angry tears. Wieser describes this poem as being one of her important poems because it "ties so much of the pain and trauma women, especially Indigenous women, experience." I agree.

Ana Mendieta, Cuban American artist, allegedly fell to her death from a 34th floor apartment balcony of artist husband Carl Andre. Neighbors heard screams before her death, but ultimately after appearing before the judge he was not charged. Mendieta's iconic work depicts bloody violence against women. In contrast, Mendieta's art also depicts herself as an integral part of the landscape where she becomes the trees and earth. It seemed as though becoming part of the landscape became her escapist solution.

> What candle do I light
> Santeria style
> to guide her home?
> To urge her ghost to cease
> its wanderings,
> its possessions of the young
> looking wide eyed and ready in the dark
> calling up butchers,
> its theatre of captivity
> by the lens of the camera,
> the ultimate selfie,
> trussing herself for slaughter and
> consumption
>
> I'm sick of being
> haunted by Ana Mendieta…

Wieser's poem begs for a solution to historical trauma and missing and murdered Indigenous women. It begs for release from the grief, sorrow, and hauntings we endure as women. What's a modern–day solution we ask? When will our lives matter? And, what's the woman's responsibility in sexual and domestic violence?

In "Mi Vida en Comancheria," we reach the safety of love and home. In Wieser's "Ghost Haikus of Comancheria," "Nopales, Hogplum, Palo Blanco, Turkey Pear, Mesquite, and Weissach," all represent the familiar surrounding landscape of home and the most recent Comanche homelands in Oklahoma. It is rich with imagery and forgotten history. Similarly, "Courtship" is a celebration of love conjuring up romantic images of a Robby McMurtry painting of Comanche love—where all anyone needs is love and a good pony.

> Hold me, Sweetheart
> Safely in your arms.
> Let me be the one you call "Honey," hey-yah
> Make here Home, if you really love me,
> Sugarpie.
> Yeh yo hey-yah, ye hyo hi yah.
> Hey-yah, hey-yah ho...

"Courtship" ends with a sweet "49" song or as Comanche describe, "the dance after the dance." Today's activists advise it's time to "take back the narratives" of our own stories, histories, songs, and celebrations that have been interpreted, explained or translated for us. Perhaps our attention was more focused on survival.

Wieser takes us on an expansive journey across Americana. The final chapter gives us an intimate glimpse into mighty love, courtship, and its miraculous healing powers. Home is a place where our surroundings are familiar, an embodiment of one's very own being. It represents a sacred place for healing.

It was an honor to write the introduction for this powerful book of poems. Readers should consider my list and relish the brilliant and provocative storytelling script. May all our journeys together be safe ones.

~Juanita Pahdopony, Lawton, Oklahoma, 2018

Forward: The Couleur of Roses: Méstizaje Historia de Tejas

Editors' Note

Roses have been used to symbolize love, sex, the feminine, hope, and even new beginnings. Interestingly, it is the rose that was one of the first flowers to be actively mixed— hybridized to create unique and differently recognized strains of roses. Kimberly G. Wieser's debut collection, *Texas... To Get Horses*, opens with the 1853 version of "The Yellow Rose of Texas," found in *Christy's Plantation Melodies*, published in Philadelphia by Edwin P. Christy.[1] Considered one of the most well-known traditional songs of the 19th century and the unofficial state song of Texas,[2] "The Yellow Rose of Texas," has a history within minstrelsy practices and is associated with miscegenation during the 1800s. A song where a rose is more than a rose, there have been various incarnations and lyrical liberties taken with the song over time. The earliest unpublished, un-authored, handwritten version is held in the archives at The University of Texas.[3] The first popularized print version of the song, located in *Christy's Plantation Melodies*, was performed within the context of Edwin Christy's blackface minstrel group: Christy's Minstrels. While minstrelsy was widespread throughout the 19th and early 20th century, it was at its most popular from 1850, right before the U.S. Civil war, until 1870, the years directly after. Minstrelsy sought to reinforce racial stereotypes and hierarchies often under the

---

[1] Dunn, J. and Lutzweiler, J. (2010). *Yellow Rose of Texas | The handbook of Texas Online | Texas State Historical Association (TSHA).*

[2] The state song of Texas is "Texas, Our Texas," written by Marsh and Gladys Yoakum Wright in 1924.

[3] Smith, C. (2013). *Early Transatlantic Writing Project | Texas History and Antebellum Slavery: The Yellow Rose of Texas: The Musical.*

guise of entertainment, sexploitation of black/mixed-race women, and demasculinization of black/mixed-race men. Christy's Minstrels includes three other botanical songs about mixed-race women in their collection.[4] Yet, what ultimately is reinforced is the continued sexualization of female bodies of color as connected to land/place within white patriarchal entertainment structures.

"The Yellow Rose of Texas," like Turtle Island itself, is wrapped within a complex history. The mythos surrounding its cult status heroine often obscures the complexities of U.S. / Mexico relations and the space Texas occupies for peoples of mixed-race/ méstiz@ ancestry in the U.S. south-by-southwest with a homogenized hegemonic narrative. "The Yellow Rose of Texas," folksong, minstrel song, and love song, has become connected to the Texas legend Emily D. West. She is often misremembered as the mythic Emily Morgan "by those who presumed her a slave of James Morgan and the 'Yellow Rose of Texas.'"[5] West's role in the battle of San Jacinto, the decisive battle in the Texas Revolution, has been speculated, mythologized, imagined, and ultimately iconized by a commemorative statue in Houston. A free woman of color, West signed a contract to work as a housekeeper for Morgan, a Texas settler and commander at Galveston during the revolution. On April 16, 1836, the Mexican Calvary took Emily, her children,

---

[4] Also included in Christy's Minstrelsy is "The Virginia Rose-Bud," "The Rose of Alabama," and "The Rose of Baltimore," wherein mixed-African descent women are likened to various flowers including roses and tobacco flowers, where they are focus of lusts, longings, and men mourning their charms and the land/state they come from. See: Dunn, J. and Lutzweiler, J. (2010). *Yellow Rose of Texas | The handbook of Texas Online | Texas State Historical Association (TSHA)*.

[5] Henson, and Margaret Swett. "WEST, EMILY D." *The Handbook of Texas Online| Texas State Historical Association (TSHA)*, 15 June 2010, tshaonline.org/handbook/online/articles/fwe41.

other servants, slaves, and people of color as prisoners. According to legend, the story is "that Emily had helped defeat the Mexican army by a dalliance with Santa Anna."[6] However, no evidence has supported this narrative except for the so-called diary of one white man. William Bollaert, an Englishman exploring Texas at the time of the battle in 1842, is credited with a July 6th diary entry saying: "The Battle of San Jacinto was probably lost to the Mexicans, owing to the influence of a Mulatta girl (Emily) belonging to Col. Morgan who was closeted in the tent with g'l Santana, at the time the cry was made."[7] However, this misrepresentation is simply hearsay appearing in the *The Day of San Jacinto* (1959). No such diary entry or any other documentation to or from Bolleart or Houston has ever been found. Moreover, ultimately, "The Yellow Rose of Texas" never had any connection to San Jacinto, Santa Anna, or Emily West —a free woman of color employed by James Morgan and taken captive during the Texas/Mexican War. Rather, the mythos around the song is the result of a writer, rumor, and "fake news" spread "so successfully... that the song and the story are forever ingrained in the public consciousness."[8]

While "The Yellow Rose of Texas" holds interest as mythos surrounding its imagined mixed-race heroine, what it does factually is open the discussion on the realities of miscegenation and post-contact Indigenous communities in the neutral zone (land on the Louisiana-Texas and Texas-Oklahoma borders) of Texas. The border between Louisiana and Texas in the 18th and 19th century was not definitively demarcated; nor so was it between Oklahoma and Texas in

---

[6] ibid

[7] Holley, Joe. "Mystery Still Surrounds 'Yellow Rose of Texas'." *Houston Chronicle*, Houston Chronicle, 1 Apr. 2016.

[8] Ibid.

the 19th century. These strips of land were often referred to
as "Neutral Ground." Historically this space became a haven
for Indians, Creoles, mixed-race communities, runaway
slaves, and outlaws. Yet, throughout history, women factored
prominently in the settlement of the parishes/counties that
sprang from the neutral ground.[9] Women's significance on
this frontier as holding cultural capital mediating between
Spanish, French, mestizos (Mexicans/Creoles), and various
tribal peoples of Louisiana, Texas, and removed tribes
within Southern Oklahoma[10] signals political and cultural
rapport grounded both in tribal tradition and a firm
understanding of settler colonial politics.[11] However, while
women were decidedly at the center of transnational
brokering within the neutral ground, the literature of the
Lone Star state often reflects a narrative expunging their
presence along with that of Blacks and mixed-Southeast
Indians, while simultaneously erasing the Indigeneity of
post-contact Indigenous/Afro-Indigenous Latinidad peoples
– Mexican, Creole, and otherwise.

Comanches, Kiowas, Caddos, and Apaches, who call
vast portions of Texas home, were heavily impacted by the
arrival of the Spanish. As Spanish presence in Texas spread,
regional trade was disrupted, "leading the Apache,
Comanche, and Kiowa Indians to migrate into the South
Plains to be nearer the supply of Spanish horses."[12] This lead

---

[9] This is particularly true within the Louisiana Creole and Indian
communities in the western Louisiana parishes of Natchitoches, Sabine,
Rapides, Allen, Calcasieu, and others with its overlap in Texas from
Harrison and Panola down to Jefferson and Galveston counties.
[10] Caddo, Quapaw, Wichita, Comanche, Choctaw, Chickasaw, Apache,
Atakapa-Ishak, Tonkawa and others.
[11] Julia Barr, *Peace Came in the Form of a Woman: Indians and Spaniards in
the Texas Borderlands.* 1-2.
[12] Klos, George. "INDIANS." *The Handbook of Texas Online* | *Texas State
Historical Association (TSHA)*, 15 June 2010.

further to processes of méstizaje within Spanish occupied areas, as Comanche, Kiowa, and Apache took mestiz@ and Native women from tribes further south into what we call Mexico. As the territory of "Texas" began to take shape, it was informed by its history of méstizaje. "Many Tejanos were descendants of mestizos. On the frontier this group rapidly became the largest segment of the population."[13] Moreover, blurring racial lines among Tejanos coupled with the lack of Anglo/European women led to an environment that encouraged Tejano men (mixed-race men) to partner or engage in barraganeria (plaçage) with Indian, African-Slave, Creole, and Mestiz@ women,[14] resulting in further multigenerational patterns and genealogies of mixing both genetically and culturally.

Into this already complex admixture are woven the additional histories of Southeastern Indian mixedbloods, Louisiana Creoles, and African Americans. Southeast Native Americans have been present in Texas from time immemorial. The Atakapa-Ishak of Louisiana and SE Texas have called and continue to call the Gulf coast of eastern Texas home, with traditional homelands running from Vermillion Bay, LA to Galveston Bay, TX.[15] Cherokees have made Texas lands home since 1807, "when a small band, probably an offshoot of the Arkansas settlements,

---

[13] Supplee, JOAN E. "MESTIZO." *The Handbook of Texas Online | Texas State Historical Association (TSHA)*, 15 June 2010.

[14] Carroll, Mark M. *Homesteads Ungovernable: Families, Sex, Race, and the Law in Frontier Texas, 1823-1860*. University of Texas Press, 2001. 12.

[15] As noted by Ishak council member Jeffery Darenesbourgh, the Atakapa-Ishak have "historically interwoven itself with African peoples who've found themselves on our lands, so much so that we have sometimes referred to ourselves as 'Creole Indians.'" See: Darensbourg, Jeffery. "Traveling Light." *SITUATE*, Situate Magazine, 13 June 2016

established a village on the Red River."[16] A number the of Cherokees known as Old Settlers, those who moved to Arkansas before the Trail of Tears, along with smaller groups of other Five Civilized descendants, eventually found their way into Texas. The most notable Cherokee migration occurred in 1819 when "Chief Bowles with sixty of his men and their families moved into Texas and settled in Caddo Indian Country... The total territory claimed by the Texas Cherokee lay between the Trinity and Sabine Rivers north of the San Antonio Road. The Texas Cherokee formed an alliance with other refugee Indians, including Shawnee, Delaware, Kickapoo, Choctaw, Biloxi, Alabama and Coushatta tribes."[17]

Cherokees, Choctaws, Chickasaws, Seminole, and Creek, whose larger populations were forcefully and brutally removed to I.T. (Indian Territory, Oklahoma), also participated in African slaveholding practices. The Chickasaw and Choctaw Nations within Oklahoma, which butted up closely to the Texas border, have shared a history of both tribal members and Freedmen (black Indian slave descendants) crossing into Texas and of Anglo-Texans and mixed-race Tejanos crossing into Chickasaw and Choctaw territory I.T. While Texas was a slave-holding state, like its neighbor to the east, it shares a complex history of miscegenation. "People of African descent were part of the population that settled Texas in the 17th and 18th centuries. This population included free and enslaved black and mixed-race people, as interracial marriage was legal and

---

[16] Lipscomb, Carol A. "CHEROKEE INDIANS." *The Handbook of Texas Online | Texas State Historical Association (TSHA)*, 12 June 2010.
[17] Cherokee Nation Cultural Resource Center. "The Texas Cherokee." *The Cherokee Hot House*, Cherokee Nation Oklahoma , 2010.

very common."[18] Louisiana Creoles, the post-contact Afro-Indigenous peoples of Louisiana, whose communities along the neutral ground had long bled into Texas, continued to migrate further into the state as U.S. expansion grew. Southeast Texas, including "the region known as 'the Golden Triangle' (the towns of Beaumont, Orange and Port Arthur) and Houston's Third Ward," is still home to many Louisiana Creole descendants and a place where Kouri Vini (Louisiana Creole) and Zydeco (Afro-Indigenous-Latinidad music of Louisiana Creoles) can still be heard.[19]

This is the fertile soil of southeast Texas: multigenerational mixed lineages rooted through Indigenous peoples, colonization, removals, slavery, and méstizaje. It is this soil that breeds news beginnings— hybridizes new roses— rosas amarillas para Tejanos. Kimberly G. Wieser's debut collection, *Texas ... To Get Horses*, blooms from this history, unfurling in all its beauty, violence, survival, and complexity.

~Rain Prud'homme-Cranford, Calgary, Alberta, 2018

---

[18] Bullock Texas State History Museum. "The African American Story | Texas State History Museum." *The Roughneck Story | Texas State History Museum*, www.thestoryoftexas.com/discover/campfire-stories/african-americans.

[19] Dhillon, Georgina. "Creoles in Texas – 'The Afro-Seminoles.'" *International Magazine Kreol*, Kreyol Magazone, 16 Apr. 2014.

The Yellow Rose of Texas (1853)[20]

There's a yellow girl in Texas
That I'm going down to see;
No other darkies know her,
No darkey, only me;
She cried so when I left her
That it like to broke my heart,
And if I only find her,
We never more will part.

She's the sweetest girl of colour
That this darkey ever knew;
Her eyes are bright as diamonds,
And sparkle like the dew.
You may talk about your Dearest Mae,
And sing of Rosa Lee,
But the yellow Rose of Texas
Beats the belles of Tennessee.

Where the Rio Grande is flowing,
And the starry skies are bright,
Oh, she walks along the river
In the quiet summer night;
And she thinks if I remember
When we parted long ago,
I promised to come back again,
And not to leave her so.

---

[20] From "The Yellow Rose of Texas," in *Christy's Plantation Melodies*, No. 2, Philadelphia, Edward P. Christy, 1853.

I. El Rio de Los Brazos de Dios—The River of the Arms of God

Méona'hané'e

I was born at the time when muscadine grapes
and wild plums
reach their fullest ripeness in Texas,
when redbirds dart across dirt roads,
grasshoppers leap suddenly from brown grass,
and stars
dance
patterns
in night sky.

I was born of mixed blood and mixed ways,
good stories
and bad,
stories people burst forth with laughter,
stories people screamed,
stories no one dared speak aloud,
whispering themselves
in shadows.

But I have never been one to give in to my enemies…
even ones who have loved me.

Dawn arrives.

I greet the Sun.
Battle.
Woman warrior.
Word weapons,
melody medicine songs,
dark harmony,
ancestral liturgies of penance.

Native Born Texan[21]
(a found poem)

Gonzales, Texas, July 10
To the Galveston News:

I see in your valuable paper
where they are trying to find the oldest native-born Texan.
I therefore take pleasure
in addressing you these few lines
in order to give you some information of my life
and of how long I have been here.

I don't know as I'm the oldest,
but feel certain I'll tally up in being the next.

My mother and a lady by the name of Mrs. McCoy
were the first two of our women
who slept on the soil of Texas,
my mother's foot the first to touch the earth here,
being first off *The Lively,*
the boat the Old Three Hundred took
to the mouth of the Brazos, then upriver.

My father came to Texas with Austin in 1822.
He settled on the Trinity.
There he put in the first ferryboat ever built
in the state of Texas.
It now goes by the name of Robbins Ferry.

He lived there twelve months,
then sold out to his brother Nat Robbins,
later the first Indian agent
of the Great Republic of Texas;
he, like my father, always held such

---

[21] Adapted from John Reed Robbin's "Native Born Texan," *The Galveston Daily News* 15 July 1904: 6.

great sway with the Indians,
back in North Carolina and Arkansas.
My father and mother moved to the Brazos.
Settled four miles north of San Felipe.
There I was born,
the 27th day of March, 1824.
In 1826, Stephen F. Austin sent
my father with a letter to the Cherokees and
Chief Fields from the Mexican government
that had talked all of us into coming here,
as they had been completely incapable of
fighting Comanches and settling the province.

Mexico's failure to keep its promises to them
had the Cherokees ready to join Edwards
in the Fredonia Rebellion.
Mexico won, and the Huacos,
peaceful allies of the pugnacious Comanches,
died one by one as they went for their morning drink
from the spring that they held holy,
making them impervious to bullets.
Us? We all stayed citizens of Mexico.
The Comanches signed a peace treaty,
and the Texas Cherokees executed
Chief Fields themselves.

But we persisted.

The first public works they had in Texas -a water mill -
was built 12 miles west of San Felipe, on Mill Creek.
Built by a man by the name of Cummings.
He received 15 leagues of land for erecting it.

I have lived under all flags;
have been in all campaigns gotten up in Texas,
except 1830.
The first gun that was fired
was fired 4 miles west of Gonzales,

on the south-side of the river,
the beginning of the Mexican War.
The people of Gonzales
have erected a large granite stone,
giving all dates.

The old settlers had a hard row to weed
when they first came here.
The closest market was Red River.
We had no post office.
All the mail came by hand.

I drank my first glass of buttermilk
out of a terrapin shell.

The first man baptized a Protestant in Texas,
defying Catholic Mexico's law,
was baptized by my uncle Isaac Reed,
in 1830 in Nacogdoches County,
where my uncle had been preaching
since he arrived.
He later formed the first church,
Old Union Baptist.

The first Methodist meeting in Texas
was held in Austin County in 1834,
Rev. Bavett being the preacher.
The first man that joined that church
was a man by the name of Rabb.

The treaty we Texans made
with the Comanches didn't hold
as Johnny-come-latelies flooded in,
and my uncle Nat ended up fighting them anyway.

Neither did the treaty my father's friend Houston signed with
them in 1844 at Tehuacana Creek...
not after Texas joined the union in 1845,

and we all became Americans once again
despite all our past efforts to the contrary,
our attempts to actually live as free men.

But such is life.

Texas was a wild place,
but God almighty,
being powerful and victorious over all things,
has made it a grand and good old place.
The health of the community is generally good.
Crops are good.

–John Reed Robbins

Texas Traces

The dry spring
white men call China
still bubbling a world ago.
Comanche Grandmothers,
wash their children in its pool,
their splashes and baby sounds
are my aubade.

When De Vaca,
gone Native,
roamed these lands,
only Lake Caddo was born.
El Rio de los Brazos de Dios—
The River of the Arms of God—
cradled Earth's Children
and ran in their veins.

The place of each emergence was Holy.

Sugar Loaf Mountain,
where the first Tonkawa
came out of the clay,
has been sliced away
by a land "owner"
tired of "tourists."

There are Old Circles
out at Ft. Hood, though,
once guarded by my old friend Randy,
part Cherokee,
part archaeologist.

My son finds bits and pieces—
birdpoints, speartips, "Huaco sinkers"—
when he hunts with his father,

but when the guy at DMV
asks him if we're "mixed,"
he says,
"*She's* Indian,"
pointing to me.

At the H.E.B.,
they think I'm either white
or Mexican
and decide upon the order of my service.

Good thing I'm not in Oklahoma.

I'd have to wait until last
if anyone of "authority"
guessed,
like the time when the Asian woman
in Oklahoma City
cheated me of a dollar of gas,
daring me with her guard dog
behind the counter
to complain,
or the time in Seiling,
accompanied by a Cheyenne,
a Kiowa-Arapaho,
and a Japanese-Italian with braids like a breed...
even the Black folks treated us like trash.

But here, en Tejas, me and the Mexicans,
we know who we are.
Some of the traces are Coahuiltec,
like graves of Ray's ancestors
in the mission courtyard
in San Antonio de Bexar,
down the street
from where he lives
in the same old barrio.

And the pictures of my great-grandparents
down near San Marcos,
with the census records
black and whiting their migration
don't lie,
though textbooks
still say
all the Cherokees in Texas
died with Chief Bowles,
all the Choctaws and Creeks took off for Oklahoma.

We still pray down here,
respect those spirits,
los antepasados,
and the ancestors of those
who traversed the Red River.
Those old Comanches.
Kiowas,
Lipans,
Wichitas,
Caddos,
Tonkawas,
Tehuacanas,
Huacos,
those old ones on the coast,
by Annette's house
and my mom's,
those Karankawas
and others
whose names
white man's story
has erased
from even our memory,
we still remember them anyway.
Nameless, they are still family.

With language unremembered,
we utter cries calling them back.

10

Lena Fair

A woman like my Stradivarius,
skin smooth brown of fine wood grain,
her waist and hips fitting my hands
as well as my fiddle.

My folks made no fuss
when I made her my bride,
unlike her aunts who complained
when her Pa married her Ma
about "that Indian woman."
She was our kind of Indian,
not a wild Comanche like
her uncles fought as Rangers.

My sweetheart was fine
and bright as creamed coffee.

Sun and hard work darkened her.
My foolish pride
broke her heart.

Couldn't stand the sharecropping, myself.
And I couldn't stand my wife working for another man.

–Cyrus Thomas Robbins

Maid in America

I am Jefferson's idea realized;
        I am not Indian.
I was the little "white" girl with
olive skin and hazel eyes who tanned "easy."
I was the teenager who tried to mask my round
face and small, slanty eyes with makeup, who wanted
her skin to be white or brown, or either one or the other,
who loved Mexican boys best,
because they looked most like her daddy.
I was the young woman asked continually
if she were Hispanic. It's hard to answer that as
        I'm not Indian.
To me, Mississippi and Alabama are places of myth;
Oklahoma is a foreign land.
But I have learned more in my life
from Old Woman than from anybody.
Even how to travel across Big Rivers.

When I was fourteen months old, my parents divorced, and I
moved in with my father's parents: Mammy and Pappy. They
worked shifts, she at the hospital, he at the oil refinery, so
Mammy's sister, Aunt Ruby, moved in to take care of me. My
Aunt Ruby bought me Indian toys, bells, dolls, beaded coin
purses. The best was Minnehaha, a leftover Black Panther doll on
which the toy company put long braids and a red and white vinyl
dress and called "Indian." Aunt Ruby made me a dress out of my
uncle's discarded khakis, machine—embroidering it with moons,
stars, the sun and tipis. She painted my face with lipstick. She
made me a tent out of a pink blanket and the dining room table.
(I never played cowboys, just Indians.)... I don't know who was
more Indian, me or Minnehaha.

Aunt Ruby was brown.
She called me little Indian sister.
        I am not Indian.

She taught me how to pick and cook poke salad,
that dewberries and wild grapes were precious things,
that tobacco was good for bee stings,
and its smoke in a child's ear for an earache or stomachache.
When I was five, she taught me how to
make change and run a cash register.
And she put me in charge of the
entire front of the convenience store.
She taught me that I was strong. I was capable.
I could do anything I had mind to.

Moon Cookie Summers
Rosebud, Texas, circa 1970s

Before we knew
how small we were
and how big the world was,
we explored fiercely.
Experience was direct,
unawed as we were by the immensity of it all.

We pedaled streets,
so hot, they would melt
in patched, black
sticky places,
coughing dirt and wheat chaff
from the baseball field we stomped up
morning, noon, and night,
me, badly,
but some like sleek brown gods and goddesses ran,
a bit of grace in the boredom of one of
the poorest counties in Texas.

Abandoned houses
full of mystery and danger,
old grey boards
glass jars and liquids
that puzzled us,
long, rotting sheets of stained beige cloth
hanging from walls and ceilings,
remnants of past-glory floral wallpapers,
hiding bad guys my dad, the cop,
later said,
ending our adventure story,
better than all the novels I consumed
from the bricked Dee Brown library
whose aging volumes had already taught me,
the scent of all good escapades was old.

We chugged twenty-five cent cans of soda water,
Big Reds or Dr. Peppers from Truvee's,
gorged from tiny brown paper sacks
full of Moon Cookies
or candy from Tasty Mart, Zip's, or Malchik's Five and Dime—
orange chewy peanuts,
Now and Laters that stuck to our teeth
in fruit-scented clumps,
Jolly Ranchers that lasted for days—
We blew green apple, pink, and grape Double-Bubble
and waited for our bubbles to burst...

Running those streets
in Texas heat,
we prayed for long, slow days at the Falls,
our only escape
after racism and the black, cracking gumbo of Texas dirt
closed Rosebud City pool.

Perfumed with repellent and the sweet, sticky sweat of children,
we swatted mosquitoes
and caught fireflies
trapped them in temporary Ball jar prisons.
Did we know?
We were watching ourselves,
brilliant beauty caught in tiny glass cells,
the unseen hands of our parents
and town, sheltering us
from the reality of what was out there,
beyond the city limits,
the gravel roads we would learn better as teenagers,
what was there, present,
right off of our very own blacktop,
but invisible to those of us who were lucky.

What I would give, today,
for a town that still held horses and chickens,

stores that children could safely walk to,
Brian Parcus cutting meat
onto the paper on the old scale
at the grocery,
for wooden cases of glass bottles,
returned for deposit,
at Aunt Aileen's place,
for a day, an hour,
with my Aunt Ruby
behind the register,
for endless dimestore afternoons,
wandering through the same toys,
fabric, miscellaneous household goods,
cooler than outside,
even with sun rays beaming through
storefront glass windows.

What I would give for a mess of fish,
cornmeal crisp,
just a few hours from swimming at Ellison's,
a pasture tank, or the river,
for some barbeque,
slightly charred at the edges,
bathed in dark red sauce,
a bowl of Homemade Vanilla,
with or without dewberry cobbler.

What I would give... for just one taste of home.

"Five foot high 'n risin'"
for Kelly, mi comadre, 07/07/07

There was high water on the Brazos
in our fortieth summer,
the summer of floods,
but you are that sandbar
that never goes under.
Both of us born near the bay
on the Gulf Coast,
we left salty water
for this small pond,
fed by a creek that was often dry.

Rakael, we took that first drink of whiskey
when we were only twelve or thirteen
hiding in the girls' bathroom
across from the gym.
That Canadian Mist you swiped
from Maurice's airplane trip stash
chased me all the way up north
over the years.
You left —then came back,
stuck with the Rosebud koolaid,
the kind that comes in aluminum cans,
and married Eduardo Salazar, who fell in love with your
Reba McIntire looks.

Lots of folks have drowned, held down in the arms of God,
that old Brazos River,
right near the Falls,
where it's supposed to be safe.
Let's hold our heads high
no matter what we have to
wade through,
no matter how high
the River gets.

Carnival Pictures

I wonder,
in this country
am I the only one holding
carnival pictures—
evidence of identity,
in this feast of flesh
we call America,
where Grandfathers
ate Grandmothers' peoples
up for dinner
with a satisfying belch
in the name of expansion?

Worn images
of women
who gave birth
and gave birth
and gave birth
when so many
of our children
died—

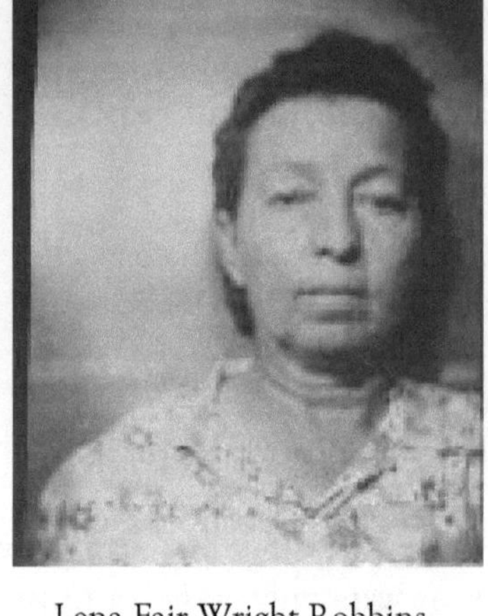

Lena Fair Wright Robbins

in their arms
in fields
on streets
with bottles in their hands.

Heavy trails
on their faces
my grandmothers' mothers
both young in their frames
above my tv
exhaustion under her laughter
exhaustion under her straight gaze
with men with no names
alone.

Did you dream me
my luxury
of complaining about *nothing*,
complaining when
my children are well
their bellies full?
Of a man who
stayed around
long enough
to find fault with?
Of sometimes passing
for white
when that privilege is *so much*,
so much more than it ought to be,
yet *I* complain,
and get by with staring,
with rocking the boat?

What unearthly ease
would this be for you
this life
the life
you
gave
me,
conceived
in your wombs and in your spirits
with sweat and imagination?

My maternal great-grandmother, Eunice
Price Hendrix Bartee, at a carnival with
two unknown men.

19

Diaspora

My Aunt Annabelle,
now *she's* a writer—
crafting poems for her sisters,
for church,
even one to sing us back together again
for the family cookbook.
She and Uncle Nelson
never had much, in terms of things.
They lived a life together, simple and moral.
In their trailer house,
there was a direct connection to God
and good food,
the mark of balanced people,
as I see it,
who discern in this unbalanced world
that Creator has kneaded us together
like dough,
equal parts of spirit and flesh.

It seems wrong to me now,
now that they're aging,
now that Uncle Nelson is dying of a stomach cancer
his actions didn't create,
now that Aunt Annabelle is laid up
with a broke foot,
now that Aunt Jessie is in the hospital
with emphysema,
like Aunt Ruby had for years
before
she crossed,
now that Mammy is lonely
and repeats herself
in her calls to me
on her "free weekend cell phone minutes,"
wrong that we're not all together.

I know they have sent us out
to conquer this new world
conjured up
by demons in business suits
on the belly of our Mother,
but it is
at times
like this
that I miss clan
and town
the most.

I should be able to be there,
for all of them,
like I should have been able to
for Aunt Ruby.
Those sisters need to be able
to be together
in one place,
surrounded by husbands, children, grandchildren, great...

Oh, women who mothered me,
who led me on grand adventures as a child,
three of you driving together simultaneously
in the front seat,
me in a spacious backseat
filled with cousins,
in those old luxurious cars of yours,
the mark of our coming up
in the world
from the poverty of your childhood,
when you were rich in togetherness,
no matter how many times you moved
from sharecropping shack to boarding house
or how many nights you went without supper.

One, though, was always the fourth sister,

a satellite
spinning out
into the world
to blaze with the trail
of your soaring
a new path
for our family.
You took turns on point.
How can I thank you properly,
when I can't even do the smallest thing
to ease your physical discomforts,
the transition
from this world to the next
one part at a time?

I am sitting here crying
in the hours before dawn
that I can't even pour you a cup
of this coffee that I've made,
scattered as we are
like something
spilt or broken
into tiny pieces
on the ground.

kitchen table refuge

kitchen table refuge particle board circle became my roof my little
home a center in the dysfunction the flying glass above me the
hard words that even though i was three and could read i
wouldn't dare use hiding from the booze and fists and feet that
my grandfather never aimed at me but that hit home anyway
hiding from the future when he would aim something more
dangerous that my grandma blocked but that hit home anyway my
imaginary friends breadcrumbs that i talked to all with names
starting with v... veronica victoria vivian vanessa almost driving
him crazy in his delirium tremors his withdrawal making him
think i'd already lost what mind i had the alcohol filled cough
elixir i spooned down him as he was "sick" trying to make him
feel better trying to take away the pain i was sane enough to hide
from circle of false wood assimilated trees reconstituted reality you
absorbed the shock of tears of kicks of stories of time and death
and i hauled you two thousand miles after my grandma passed
scarred with scratches with burns from cigarettes and hot spoons
my uncle dropped in a cloud of black tar i can't let go of you
anymore than i can let go of the good food and bad memories the
family recipes i change to suit my needs those of my children
none of whom have names starting with v anymore than i can let
go of the taste of laughter mixed with tears

Ghosts

My ghosts?

                                They follow me everywhere.
                                I feed them.
                                Offer smoke.
                                Tell their stories,
                                renew their lives,
                                and call them "Spirit,"
                                call them "Grandpa,"
                                call them "Grandma,"
                                draw them closer,
                                tugging gently
                                on the cords of light
                                that bind us.
                                Family can be remade.

I sing,

                                my voice
                                undulating outward
                                wavelike
                                from This Center
                                and the ripples
                                wash over my Sisters.

One

                                Two
                                Three
                                Four

They echolocate,

                                Return.

Sagwu

                                Tali
                                Tso'i
                                Nvgi

Together

                            We are strong

Igido
for Kim Shuck

I have to read them
over and over
your songs
chant them
till they fill
empty torn corners
inside my belly
and rib cage
like cotton batting
in your beaded creatures
till they whip stitch
my frayed edges
tight safely
Sister-Mender
word render
me whole
tattoo my
real visage
in sparkling Czech glass
with your singing.

The difference between
the downside of diaspora
and the upside of the clan system
is that you, my Sister,
would be here,
drawing your stitches
sinew tight,
or rather
we'd both be back there
where we belong
not just to each other

but to a circle
of seven mountains and a mound
unleveled by a farmer's plow.

The Real Americana

I am the American Woman,
and I am every bit as dangerous and wonderful
as the singers have said.
You may have more important things to do
than spend your time going on with me,
but even if I've been married fifteen times,
you'll still love me anyway.

I am democratic in my loving—
men and women,
Indian, Italian, Irish, Chicano, Chicana,
Black, Jewish, Cuban,
and even straight-up Redneck White Boys,
I have been egalitarian about
these things, about where
I have allocated my affections.
Sisters and Lovers and Friends and Brothers,
I have a hard time being selfish with.

American Women get a good dose
of the desire to be a martyr
at a
very
young
age.

I have conceived children in the
back of a green '79 Ford Thunderbird
and in my German great-grandmother's
hand-me-down bed.
I have nursed them in tipis
and in shopping malls.
I have raised them
with men by myself
and

by myself by myself.
And I even, on occasion,
have allowed others
to help.

I can fry chicken,
make jerky,
cook a mean chili,
a serious stew,
and make
the
world's
best
frybread.

My children have drunk enough
Kool-Aid to dye them permanently red, yellow,
orange, green, and blue. The identities of their fathers
affect the color of their skin less than what I weaned them on.

I've been a brunette,
a blond,
a red head.
And I've discovered that
all it takes to snag a man is
the irresistible
aroma of
estrogen
and
hairspray.
A checkbook
to pay for the pizza
is simply
a bonus.

The things I can do with
bacon
are mere parlor tricks.

I can
catch a fish,
clean a deer,
write a love poem,
perform emergency
C-sections,
tracheotomies,
vasectomies,
and acrylic
my best friend's
nails.

If it means feeding my children,
I can sell you anything,
and you'll pay my price—
wisdom, dope, lipstick,
a beer,
or a plate of food,
even my body,
but you'll never,
never own
my spirit,
never
put a UPC on
my soul.

I'll feed you
if
you're hungry,
shelter you
if
you're cold.
I'll fix
your broken heart.
And I'll break it
in two
again
if

necessary,
because
my children
must survive.
It's the first commandment
of my Great Mother.

You can call me
a bitch
if
you want to,
Just don't call me a whore
or any other kind of capitalist
because
if
you think
I'll be
your sucker,
you're dead
wrong
mister.

II. Spanglish is the Language of the 21st Century

Rearview Mirror 2007

"Hecho en México,"
a little tin cut-out
dancer
dangling
in many colors,
"de colores…"
decorating him
his huge hat,
sombrero enorme,
red stripe
yellow and green spots
on silver
blue stripe,
chin strap azafrán,
face la color de rosa,
his leotard plata,
one dot, azul, above
another below
his cerise belt.
Pomegranate sleeves
blossom out,
purple sashes
over his arms
and parti-colored puffed cuffs.
Four-banded legs—
Verde-amarillo-rojo-amarillo—
tiny crimson feet.
A tie-died
trainwreck of a Sacred Clown dancing,
swinging from the rearview
mirror
of a '69 Aztec Aqua Mustang
Mach 1 fastback,
driving from El Paso
to the Mescalero Rez,

to Chaco,
Casa Grande,
on a dark, desert highway,
with more dust than cool wind
in our hair,
sage brush lining
a path from Aztlán
all the way down
to Chiapas,

down
to the calendar
ticking like a clock,
a heart,
it reads,
"Five years before the hour."

Right Fist Up

With my right fist up
I bring this crowd to a roar—
Peace and Unity
Peace and Unity
Peace and Unity
Peace and Unity

With my right hand forward
I send you the sign of
Peace...
Peace be with you.

Make love,
not war
our mommas
and daddies
used to say
in the seventies
when they were cool
when they were real people
with real ideals
and not sold out yuppies
burnt up junkies
prostitutes to the establishment
or to their own baby-booming
eternal and infantile need
a needle in an arm
or in the heart of a value
pumping society's smack...
toilet paper
ice
and air conditioning.

Now it's cell phones
and personal organizers

and pcs, macs, laptops, and internet accesses
we let the man convince us we just got to have
hum-u-vs, nice tennis shoes
And some bling around our necks.

Can somebody tell me something?
What's the answer?

Is there anyone out there who even knows the question?

Where did you go?
Beautiful People of my childhood
my long-haired cousins
and their friends with fros
my dad looking something like a Beatle
and driving a VW
even him wanting change
before he got jaded.

But here I am getting old,
and I'm not getting that way
Winston Churchill said,
"Any man who is not a liberal at 18 has no heart.
Any man who is not a conservative at 30 has no brain."
I say, but you gotta be a man first.
Or a wo-man,
a Hu-man,
Real People,
like the old folks said.
People:
We have got to start loving each other.
We have got to see past lines of color
to see it is not a matter of race or ethnicity
but a matter of have and have not—
If you don't have, those that do have
are going to make sure you don't—

And still

I know
we
Americans
are all
Rich

We suck up resources of Mother Earth.
We put food embargos on children in other lands
starve them to death
and if they survive
if someone is appalled enough at us to fight back—
this monster still keeps eating.

With my right fist up
With my right hand forward
I am begging...

Listen.

U-ne-ga

for Leo Hernandez, Taxi Cab Poet extraordinaire,
Puerta Vallarta, Jalisco, Mexico

Abuelita del pacifico,
Grandmother Pacific,
tu eres muy hermosa y peligrosa.
You are very beautiful and very dangerous.
Yo te amo.
I love you.
Madre del Mar, del Maiz, y de la Tierra.
Sea Mother, Corn Mother, Earth Mother.
Madre nuestra de Guadalupe,
Our Lady of Guadalupe,
muchas gracias por tu ayuda, por tu gracia,
 thank you so much for your help, your grace,
y por todo Puerto Vallarta.
and for all of Puerto Vallarta.
Te doy gracias por esta gente,
I give you thanks for this People.
mis parientes,
my relatives,
y por toda mi familia,
and for all of my family,
los Indios de Norteamerica.
the Indians of North America.

Gracias por las huellas de mis Antepasados,
Thank you for the footprints of my Ancestors,
los Venados,
the Deer
que estan en la playa,
which are on the beach,
el mercado,
in the market
en todas partes,
in all places

en mi corazon
in my heart
y en mi alma.
in my soul.

Vuelve,
Return
Madre nuestra,
Our Mother
danos tu luz
and give us Light
y juntanos
and join us
para que haya paz y unidad.
in Peace and Unity.

Somos Una Raza

we are the children of rape
of grandmothers
and babies sold for pleasure
of Octoroons bred for it and auctioned off in mockery
of the Monsters' own daughters'
legitimate prostitution by marriage to son-of-a-bitch
cannibal preying on human flesh of bondage
all the children of tears
that have fallen
and crystallized
into "civilization"
that buys us each
individually out
and carries out
a foreign policy
based on
made up
borders
artificial
separations of people
ordered by
artificial
separations
of
time

    while nearly seven million children starve to death each year...

Where are you my Beautiful Minds,
My Beautiful People?

Brother
Sister
Son
Daughter

Momma???
Daddy???
Auntie???
Uncle???

Somos una Raza
We are one Race
La Raza de Gente
The Human Race
De Gente de la Tierra
The People of the Earth
Nuestro Madre
Our Mother
La Raza de Gente
The Human Race
De Gente del Dios
The People of God
Nuestro Padre
Our Father
Whatever we name them...
however we
weak
human beings
try to conceive
the Unconceivable
the Ineffable
the Divine
the Divine that has told us all the same thing,
"People, Love one Another."

We have got to get
our act
together.

Somos una Raza.

LOW-RI-DER

Brown-skinned boys of my youth
how you took my breath away
with your beauty
your strength
that moment of perfection
in life
when skin
is taught
cheekbones and noses cut of stone
faces like
masked Aztec dancers
arms and legs
like steel bands
you
coiled just as tight
the fire
of man
at the moment of ripening

mi corazón
todavía se detiene brevemente
en esa imagen
cogida en tiempo
las mujeres
le amarán
por siempre
para ser que hermoso
apenas una vez,
mis amantes

it is
always
summer
where you live
in my mind

the texas
air
is wet
in the night
and your arms,
your lips,
are mine

Para Minerva

Sirena, nadadora con los delfínas,
Mermaid, swimmer with dolphins,
la belleza de su alma
the beauty of your soul
llena los cuartos de su casa.
fills the rooms of your house.
En los ojos de su hija se refleja,
It is reflected in the eyes of your daughter,
y en la sonrisa de su esposo cuando él mira sobre usted.
and in the smile of your husband when he looks at you.
 "Mi casa es su casa,"
"My house is your house,"
usted dijo,
you said,
y usted lo significó verdad.
and you truly meant it.
Usted es una buena mujer,
You are a good woman,
una buena marida,
a good wife,
una buena madre,
a good mother,
una buena amiga.
a good friend.
Tengo suerte de haberte conocido.
I am lucky to have met you.
Gracias por ser usted.
Thank you for being you.

Olvídese del pasado,
Forget the past.
Sueños dulces ideales del océano,
Dream sweet dreams of the ocean,
flotación en ondas de la paz
floating on waves of peace

43

en los mares azules de la serenidad.
in blue seas of serenity.
Haga las nuevas memorias en las aguas del amor de su familia.
Make new memories in the waters of your family's love.
Nunca me olvidaré de su amabilidad y amistad,
I will never forget your kindness and friendship,
y volveré siempre para atesorarlas una vez más.
and I will always return to treasure them once more.

A Song to Tell Robert Bly How We Do This
In My Language

My 'skin kin the ants
begin again the dance
A-ga-sga—it is raining.

Antelope pokes a hole a world below,
the new sky cries,
People emerge— it is raining.

The soldiers crowd the shivering hungry;
in a pen intended for cows a child dies,
from the eyes of the Ani' Yun'wiya—it is raining.

A man lifts his hands to the East,
the Grandmothers consult regarding blessings,
the dust returns from wind to earth—it is raining.

A white-washed church strains to reach the sun in Chiapas,
blood and brain stain its walls fresh from death,
the soil keeps drinking a five-hundred year old shot—it is raining.

The voices of my ancestors thin through brine
as they sing and flash in vast Atlantic,
a storm roars at sea, and I am born, not from shell, but their
bones and dreams—it is raining.

Una Canción para Decir Robert Bly Cómo Nos Hacer Esta en Mi Lengua[22]

—una traducción para Ana Flor Cotzojay Yoc

Mis parienties sufrientes las hormigas
reanudan el baile arábigas
A-ga-sga[23]—está lloviendo.

Antílope atiza un agujero de un mundo quebrado más abajo.
El nuevo cielo llora;
gente sale—está lloviendo.

Los soldados recogen de los hambrientos temblando;
en un corral para vacas muere un niño.
Desde los ojos de las Ani Kituwah[24]—está lloviendo.

Un hombre levanta sus manos a la Orientes.
Las Abuelas Antepasadas hablar entre sí mismos con respecto a las
bendiciones para nosotros.
El polvo regresa de viento a la tierra—está lloviendo.
Una iglesia, pintado de blanca, cepas llegar al La Sol en Chiapas.
Sangre y cerebro manchar sus paredes frescas de la muerte.
El suelo sigue bebiendo un quinientos años trago—está lloviendo.

---

[22] El poema fue inspirado por una conferencia impartida por el famoso poeta gringo Robert Bly en la Universidad de Baylor. Cuando Bly informaron a una audiencia de jóvenes poetas que deberían estudiar mitos europeos como no había nada en las Américas más de quinientos años de antigüedad, estaba furioso. Como una mujer mestiza, sabía que mis antepasados indios tenían conocimiento mucho mayor que eso. También había estado pensando sobre la masacre de Acteal de Las Abeyas y cuánto los pueblos indígenas tenemos en común por genocidio histórico y actual. Me acordé de historias sobre niños Cherokee que murieron en El Camino de las Lágrimas. Elegí la forma ghazal simulacros como Bly estaba favoreciendo a lo mismo en el momento. La ghazal auténtico es las forma Islámica. aunque Bly se apropió y modificado. Cuando lo leí a él tras bambalinas la noche siguiente, sentí que había contado golpe sutilmente lo corrigiendo.

[23] En el lenguaje de los indios Cherokee, A-ga-sga significa está lloviendo.

[24] Ani-Kituwah es el nombre de los Cherokees por sí mismos.

Las voces de mis ancestros estrechan, son delgada a través de
salmuera
como cantan y destellan en vasto Atlántico.
Ruge una tormenta en el mar, y yo nací, no de concha,
pero de sus huesos y sus sueños—está lloviendo.

Livin' in the Day of Che.com

Che—

I would have loved you
if I'd had the chance,
Dog Soldier for the people,
indigenous hero
who died for us
while others
played
the La Raza Judas.

Instead,
I wear your image
plastered
across my bosom,
yours,
Geronimo's,
some random Apaches Homeland Security Agents',
Sitting Bull's,
Sub-Commandante Marcos',
Emiliano Zapata's.

But
even my "meior morir de pie" shirts
are sellouts,
just like my camo pants from the mall,
maybe made by a Chinese child-slave
or a man in a monsoon in Mumbai,
peddling away
under a tarp
in the rain.

Just
like this book.

Today,
our ideals
come with a price tag
and ironies;
we don't know
how
to be
Free.

This Revolution
will not be fought
in chanclas,
with cell phones,
texting each other
about our rendezvous
with destiny.

The layers of plastic
will peel back,
reveal themselves
to be the blood
of giants.
We will walk
barefoot,
in moccasins
or huaraches,
our toes finally set loose
in kinesthetic balance.

We won't feel the sting
of the nuns' rulers
when we take
the hands
of our brothers,
crippled.
We'll pull them
behind us
if we have to

on travois
if their amputations are too severe.

We'll leave behind
the excess
possessions
that trap us,
carry each other along.
There won't be room
for plasma screen TVs
on this journey,
and I'm sorry, boys,
but your video
game systems
will be useless without them.

I'll have to toss out
my laptop
and
all my books,
make
new oral
traditions
'cause
this war
we are fighting
is real,
not an electronic illusion
with virtual enemies.

Like the Aztec prophets said it would be,
Anahuac is back, baby,
because here has always
been here,
and we have always been us.
We have only
to recognize it and believe.

Azul de Yoeme

Un tono de azul escapa me,
A shade of blue escapes me,
uno que sólo
one which is only
he visto en reflexiones
seen in reflections
y en mis sueños
and in my dreams

En impetuosas corrientes de la lluvia,
In rushing streams of rain,
o en el destello de una chuchillo
or in the flash of a knife
corte a través del aire como algunos raro mariposa
cutting through the air like some rare butterfly
en el corazón del sacrificio
into the heart of the sacrifice

En la piel translúcida de un espíritu de montaña baile,
In the translucent skin of a mountain spirit,
vestido con falda y tocado de Geronimo,
dressed in the skirt and headdress of Geronimo,
me roban en mi sueño
stealing me in my dream
a los catorce años tiernos
at fourteen tender years

Lo huelo en la sangre de una estrella
I smell it in the blood of a star
fluyendo en las venas de mis hijos,
flowing in the veins of my children,
intento captar
I try to grasp it
como la imagen de mi amante caminando frente a un espejo
like the reflection of my lover walking past in a mirror

51

Pero todavía tengo que verlo en una flor
But I have yet to see it in a flower
o una roca en mi andar en el camino de vida
or a rock on my path of life
o en el ojo de un bebé nacido hablando,
or in the eye of a baby born talking,
hablando del futuro...
speaking the future

"Porque Por Ella Algunos, Sin Saberlo, Hospedaron Ángeles"

Angels are awkward in human bodies,
but when they are naked,
you should clothe them.
When they are hungry,
you should feed them.

I eat with homeless men
in strange cities,
take them to breakfast,
give restaurateurs indigestion
with insistence on humane humanity.
I discomfit
as I comfort.

When they are hungry,
you should feed them.

Aren't we all hungry for something?
Aren't we all love-hungry children
starved
for a safe stable?
A Rock of Ages?
Some cleft?

I've been starving for something.
I've been thirsting for something.
I've been trapped in self-erected jail cells.
I've let people hold keys.

Angels visit for reasons,
not the least of which is our own emancipation.
They're just awkward in human bodies.
I wonder how they handle the smell,
if the stench of our collective corporeal guilt

is a diversion from paradise?
When they breathe,
you should love them.

You shouldn't shelter guests in prisons.
Child angels in garrisons
cry in the night.
God hears them
above the fattened whispers of men muttering gluttonous wishes
swathed in Egyptian cotton
reeking of blood and frankincense.

Angels arrive often at thresholds,
are turned forthwith.

They come back,
strange flesh weighting down their familiar feathery blonde curly
sparkling white souls.

Angels are lame, blind, deaf, dumb, crazed,
autistic spacecases.
They have to be to love us,
to keep trying
despite our selfish little natures,
our smallnesses of spirit.
Our meannesses.

We let our hunger maim us.
We are so stingy,
we won't even feed ourselves properly.
We wrap ourselves in Jesus,
cleanse ourselves in blood,
and roll in dirt like pigs.

We are NOT Kosher.
WE are not fit for human consumption.
We aren't fit for coyotes, buzzards, and worms
who no longer feast on our poisoned and

preserved, preserved, preserved
corpses.
The American Condition?
Los Estados Unidos crowded,
strange cities, strange flesh...
We are rotten.

But still,
angels come back to us, The Door Turners,
The Catfish Eating Rock Throwers,
The Washed Unwashed.

"Then the King will say to those on His right, 'Come, you who are
blessed of My Father, inherit the kingdom prepared for you from
the foundation of the world...'"

We expect mercy and privilege.
We want to be The Favorite Son,
The Teacher's Pet,
—Oh Rabbi, Oh Abba, My Father—
we want to be
The Altar Boy,
The Good Girl
when our stench comes
neither from our nether regions
nor our mercury-laden, PCB-ridden, radiated lobster and shrimp-
tinged breath,
but our putrid human hearts.

We host angels, unawares.

'Cause You Know When You Hear That
Nickleback Song You Always Think of Me,
Vato Loco...

Norte del Rio Rojo,
I am mythically single
and ever beautiful,
and married Mexican men
back home
go to confession
and get the standard
ten Hail Marys from
the priest
at St. Anne's
for having
dirty thoughts
about me.

That priest
is getting tired
of hearing my name,
thinks
I
am Babylon
of legend.

He doesn't have
memories
of me
on my bicycle,
browned with cinnamon freckles dusting my nose,
sun-streaked hair
and
'70s blue, sports shorts
with the white trim
that v'd up the side,
riding by when

you
were on breaks
from CCD,
or
of me,
black and rhinestone bodysuit—
órale—
shining under
stadium lights
at Cougar Field,
tossing a baton
in the air,
catching it
sometimes.

Here, in Oklas,
I order tacos
from the truck
in Spanish
because I miss you.
I butter my tortillas
in restaurants,
y una de mis hermanas indias
con el esposo Mejicano,
she says,
"You are *such*
a Mexican."

I laugh
and say,
"Not since 1836.
But I was a captive
once...
Straight Loquita."

III. Crossing the River

"And Texas is the place I'd dearly love to be
But all my ex's live in Texas..."
from "All My Ex's Live in Texas," *Ocean Front Property*,
recorded by George Strait, 1987

Na he dum[25]

i am not your eco-fairy,
i am a revolutionary,
not an exotic temptress,
not your identity witness,
not mystic stoic,
soy un indigenista poet,
worn-out jeans and a t-shirt,
not braids and a buckskin skirt,
i'm not scared of your stereotype,
i'm not scared of all your hype,
i'm not scared of the american king,
i'm not scared of the damned right wing,
i'm winning.

i'm a daughter of the ancient ones,
a singer to a female Sun,
sprung forth from of a pyramid of bones,
a worshiper with wood and stones,
in sacred darkness i breathe my prayers
over the current state of world affairs
wrapped in cedar incense smoke
i plead mercy for the sick joke
we've made of living.

i'm not scared of my own meat,
fragile shell on broken feet,
i'll be far across the river
when coyote's belly starts to quiver,
transforms a piece of dripping flesh,
before the worms, while i'm still fresh,
into canine scat and chasing rabbits
(or stealing wives, his *favorite* habit)
i'm fine with being a tree,
as fine as i am with being me,

---

[25] Cheyenne language for "I'm telling the truth."

i learned it off my Grandmas.

in the meantime, i'm gonna start some shit,
pick a fight and not run away from it,
pull out all the stops
give this world all i got
like an illegal shotgun blowing verbs
i don't care who it disturbs
my ak 47 mouth
my texas ass from way down south
my mixed up country and ndn drawl
my 'I thank sos," "fixin tas," and "y'alls,"
my "buenos," "graciases," y 'mijas,"
mis "besa mi colas" and "aye le chingas,"
i'm a polyglot of all i seen,
all i've eaten, all i've been,
and now you're of me

Ten Things That Would Have Been Different if I Had Shot You and Gone to Prison (Upon Doing Laundry and Finding a Receipt for Flowers You Bought Her with My Money)

1. Both the quality and quantity of the time I spent with my children would have been limited.
2. I would have had much of my life controlled by others, whether they were police, lawyers, judges, elected officials, wardens, guards, or lovers.
3. I likely would have become romantically entangled with violent perpetrators because of my codependent tendencies, and those perpetrators would have likely subjected me to alternating emotional abuse and false senses of security in being "loved."
4. Doubtless, I would have been subject to verbal abuse.
5. I probably would have been raped, again, more than once.
6. I also probably would have gotten regularly beaten.
7. Occasionally, I might have fought back and out maneuvered my abuser as I defended myself.
8. Perhaps, I would have even found a sick sense of pride in the scars I left behind as I defended myself.
9. My life might have actually been at risk on a number of occasions.
10. Nothing.

Kokopelli is Your Real Father
for Marley

Kokopelli is your real father
some call him alien
some call him mountain spirit dancer
he inhabited the body of the one we call your father
after all this time
I'm going to tell you the same story
it will drop down through years
trickle through cracks in rock
through holes in hearts
reach you
awaken you
stir in you what is still
break your human skin
the mask at that holds you in
free you from that chrysalis
let you fly
show us mere humans that
you
my girl
are a demigod
you
my girl
are a superhero
you
my girl
will save us
as you save yourself
from lies
they tell you
    you can't
you tell you
    you can't
but
you

can
my confession says
you can
frees you
from the tales
others tell
of your origin
stories holding you back
from your own beauty
your own power
confuse you with their screams
and mute your solo rising up
from your throat
to reach the very ear of
God

This is your story

Sweet Brown Honey

I like bullshitting fools
who break all the rules.
I like to watch their tries
to build platforms of lies
to stand on
from which
to pontificate.
I like to watch them strut
'n try their luck,
shake their ass,
share their grass,
decline,
conjugate,
and
copulate—because some days,
it's a good day
to fuck a signifying clown

I like
artists and activists,
warriors and pacifists,
creating their rhymes,
eyeing some prime,
anticipating sublime
moments
in mon
chambre à coucher.

Voulez–vous coucher avec moi ce soir.
Voulez–vous coucher avec moi—

I like the window in
to all their sin,
their trying to win
lopsided battles

that the y splash
on paper,
on canvas,
staking their belts to the ground
in concrete warzones,
making *all* of it
more beautiful.

I like to float like the moon
in the sky of a room,
a thick-haunched doe
watching hunger rise slow,
looking for and taking
the best hunter.
I like being stalked
and serenaded,
evoked
and painted,
being prayed to
and chased
while being evasive,
then luring them on in for the kill—
because I have finally,
after all this time,
figured out the one thing
that bad boys
are
good
for.

I like them sniffing my skirt
spitting phrases and words,
like "love"
and "I am in touch with my feminine side"
and "investing in property"
and "concentrating on my career."
I like their surprise
and to look in their eyes

when they ultimately figure out,
I was just in it for the nookie
'cause some turnabout is fair play, mother fucker,
which is exactly all any of them really wants to be.
So yes, I'll make you some tea,
let you be what you be,
crawl in my bed,
have it go to your head,
almost drown
in my pleasured sounds,
get yourself lost

and your signals all crossed
nearly go blind
and out of your mind
at the image of my naked splendor
beneath you...
and then I'll hold you up
while I walk you out the door.

Suggested Dialogue for Dealing with His
Sublimated Paracolonial Intergenerational
Postraumatic Stress Disorder that Causes Secret
Misogynistic Tendencies, Often Disguised by NDN
Men as "Ugg. Me Warrior. Ugg, Me Being
Traditional," When He Knows That Ain't Tradition
—for All My Rez-Sistas from Way Back

1. "You know, there's something twisted deep inside you. I'm
gonna use something I learnt oft an ole Diné lady. I'm gonna take
a crystal and look through it all over you till I find that twisted
spot, but I just betcha, it's in your heart or your balls. Then, when
you're sleeping, I'm gonna use that middle, reptilian part of my
mind, and I'm gonna reach deep inside you and untwist it." [a]

2. "Honey, I think we need to go to counseling." [b]

3. "Get a fucking job for a change of pace, will you? I don't care if
you think it's selling out or not. I've got no choice. I do it. Your
mother does it. Your sisters do it. Why the fuck can't you do it?
You might actually feel good about yourself and not have shit to
take out on me!" [c]

4. Silence. Simply continue what you are doing. Get up, make
breakfast, make lunches, dress children, send them to school, get
dressed, go to work, go by the store and get some food, come
home, pick his dirty clothes up off the floor and wash them,
gather up the dirty dishes from all over the house, wash them,
cook supper, see if the kids have done their homework and help
with that while finishing cooking supper, feed everyone, clean
kitchen, bathe children, dry those clothes you forgot about, put
the kids to bed. Get some if you can even if you can't enjoy it
because you're too tired but after all, you love him, and he's so
good-looking, and half the girls on the rez are still chasing him,
and after all, you won, he's your man, he sleeps in your bed every
night, and he's sooo good lookin, and he still looks like a god in

his regalia, just floating around the arena out there he dances so smoooooothhhhhh...[d]

5. "Six foot under, mutha fucker. This is bullshit, and I'm tired of it." [e]

a. Usually, with this approach, you'll be accused of being a witch, or he'll at least look at you real funny. *Either way, he will leave you for a twenty-one year old girl who doesn't know any better or is just a drunk little slut.

b. This statement often elicits commentary about how you have too much education, about how you talk to your sisters too much, or about how you watch way too much daytime TV talk shows. See * on footnote "a" above.

c. Just call the ambulance ahead of time, stupid, mouthy bitch.

d. See * on footnote "a" above.

e. With this option, if you act fast, you might get off on insanity, particularly if you have a stack of emergency room records for mysterious falls, etc., or you could serve some serious time. If you don't act fast, you could serve some time for terroristic threats, plus, see * on footnote "a" above. If you have really good sisters and act fast, however, you just might get away with it. Make sure your sisters haven't been snagging your man first.

Sick of Being Haunted by Ana Mendieta

I am sick of being haunted by Ana Mendieta,
her perpetual, frozen, iconic victim status.
She makes me feel raped.
She makes me feel beaten.
She makes me feel choked.

She makes me more fearful,
more a doe in the headlights,
the subject in the spot,
than do the guilty millions of perpetrators
walking down the world's streets,,
down her dark allies
and empty parking lots,
or shaking a newspaper open in a cozy room by a soft light
who have on their minds nothing
or some particular and fetishized victim
other than myself.

I am sick of being scared by Ana Mendieta.
She terrorizes me more than Jackson's visage on a twenty,
more than a fleeting memory of Hernando de Soto,
more than the snap of the whip fresh on the flesh
of la mujer salvaje.
Él es Dios.
Submit and be saved.

Mendieta offers herself up,
makes me choose—
am I *her*
or am I the scopophilic source of her suffering?

I am sick of being raped by Ana Mendieta.
She makes bruises rise to my skin.
She puts hands around my throat,
stops my breath.

She starts that tick tick tick ticking of my heart,
that familiar panic surging up from my belly
at smell of whisky and cigarettes on close breath
or an insistent touch by a drunken man,
however glancing.

I just want Ana Mendieta to,
for heaven's sake,
put on her clothes,
stay off of balconies,
stop bending over
and acting like she likes it.

I am sick of being held back, tied down, all bondaged up,
incapacitated by Ana Mendieta.
That gran zorruta locks me up inside my home,
jails my sisters in apartments,
leaves girl children in short skirts
shaking and trapped in their own bodies.
That artista de la puta
bounces my head on a linoleum floor,
holds me up and
throws me against the wall
so many times I lose count
though the technician doesn't lose count later
examining the X-rays.
My scars are visible
and indivisible.
There's nothing secret about the dryness in my mouth
and tremor of my hand on the doorknob.

Ana Mendieta leaves me vulnerable,
inside
and
out.

I don't need this voyeuristic mierda.
This repeated staging of her death.

This dress rehearsal of intimate and violent violation.
I don't need your curation
and recitation
of her practiced tragedy.
I don't need your necro-pornographic prurient
academic dissection
of her inverted Land O'Lakes Butter Maiden
take it all,
no really, take it all,
pose.

When I die,
my story will be sung by the trees
that grow from my bosom,
by the ants that gently free my bones.
You don't vicariously own
my victim narrative,
can't take my survivor story
and eroticize it to make yourself
feel special
and sensitive
and oh so liberal.

I need no settler-colonial savior,
neither priest nor nun
of the ivory tower,
to elevate my suffering through study.
I don't need a cadre of my friends
to start a movement,
to indict the guilty,
to find my Carl Andre.

They are *all* guilty.
We are all guilty.
Humans are a wreck of a creation.
What *was* God thinking?

I wonder what Ana Mendieta

looked like at her first communion.
Did she feel Ivory clean
in her veil and white dress
in Castro's Cuba?
Did she admire her brown skin,
her legs and arms emerging in Cubano sunshine
like plants from Earth Mother
who would nestle her repeatedly
someday in her photos
and gather her in closely in death,
absorb her into universe,
absolve her from pain
of leaving her familia,
her warm island mother land
for coldness of an orphanage
in Los Estados Unidos?

What candle do I light
Santeria style
to guide her home?
What prayer do I whisper
to urge her ghost to cease
its wanderings,
its possessions of the young
looking wide eyed and ready in the dark
calling up the butchers,
its theatre of captivity
by the lens of the camera,
the ultimate selfie,
trussing herself for slaughter and consumption?

I'm sick of being haunted by Ana Mendieta...

Oklahoma Two-Step

Tonight,
after my neighbor
danced from room to room
in her half of our duplex
in that frolic
called domestic violence,
the white cop
danced around the subject
at hand,
pointing out her 'dark' skin and
children's foster-care history,
then questioned assuming answers about nonexistent alcohol
instead of saying out loud,
"Just another
Indian woman who got her ass beat."

In *this* dance contest,
the system is stacked
against
you
despite
the stake
you place
for your survival,
risking
calling the cops
grasping an invisible,
impotent VPO shield
painted with war stories of
of surviving poverty and DHS.

I thought about
the weakness of English,
its inability to protect us,
to nuance

between
this category
and
Jingle Dance,
Fancy Shawl,
Women's Traditional,
Stomp Dance,
Bole Maru
Sun Dance,
Back and Forth,
cutting loose in the club,
and
disrobing for money,
all the
ways
NDN women
have danced
to save
our children's lives
and our own.

I thought about this personal war dance
and
the battles
for religious freedom,
for ceremonial dance,
reflected on facets of
Sacrifice—
all the food and
water we've done without willingly in prayer,
each shawl fringed,
each quilt pieced,
each dish prepared,
the precious turtle shells saved up for shakers,
the nights of beading each moccasin by dim light,
of painstakingly appliquéing regalia...
and
the shame

endured
in survival,
in desperate acts
of salvation.

I think of little girls
like mine
whom we bring into the Circle,
think of
her face
when she won
her first tiny tots in Ft. Worth,
of her blanket tail
dancing for Brave Dogs,
of her tiny stick in the Beaver Dance
for that Bundle,
of her learning the relationship
between Sacrifice and Dance,
cooking at Ft. Belknap with her sister
while that old woman
broke free from her burden
dancing around that Sacred Lodge...

I think of all that
and of our dances,
our lives,
me
and all their Aunties.

I worry
about
lack of shame,
too much shame,
shame on me,
shame on you.
What a shame
it all is.

It made me
happy last night
at least to see
our little girls
dancing innocently
and shamelessly
to
a video game beat,
unbeaten
by the "incident"
or the haunting presence of
the badged and holstered invader
called in to
"save" us all.

How, this morning,
with the new Sun and all its promises,
will we place our feet?
How will we maneuver survival
as She dances across the sky?
When She stops to dine with her daughter,
where will we be leading ours?

Cihuamazatl to Oquichcoyotl
(Deer Woman to He-Coyote)

Abused, misused, misconstrued…
I am no longer
deer in your headlights,
mother fucker.
When I play that role,
it's for *my* amusement,
not yours,
and I sprout hooves
and hairy ankles,
bent at odd angles,
a fluffy white tail—
watch out.

I am a daughter
for the Leaving People
who never
bled innocents.
We would not
play
the old and sacred Ball Game
surrounded by the
rotting, wide-eyed heads of the Dead.
We perfected instead The Little Brother of War.

Ishtaboli
rose
out of
Nanih Waiya,
scratched and bloodied,
willing warriors venture
to the Bonepicker
plucked
by
Holy Chance

77

to journey West.
But you,
you...
Epic Carnivore—
I *saw* you eat
my sisters.
You are
still picking
meat
out
of
Coyote teeth,
Los Dentes...
Clad in deerskin
you enter
the Ball Court
Your bedposts
are
Skull Racks, Tzompantli.

You will not
see my haunches quiver,
nor smell my grassy breath,
taste Spring Rebirth,
blossoms of wild onions
in my blood,
—remembrance—
necklace
of human gut
flowering
about
your scruffy
neck,
staggering drunk
with Blood
atop
Pyramid, Panopticon, Penthouse suite.

Moundbuilder

Naked, tattooed,
cloaked in Fire Macaw,
layered with turquesa, malachita,
freshwater pearl,
Sweat of the Sun,
Tears of the Moon,
I rise from ash,
bone ear spool,
red mud
we writhe
and bathe
in,
washing ourselves
back to
Mississippi,
Alabama,
emerald forest,
birdsong,
panther scream
in sweet misery,
her heat,
her need.

Pleasure is you,
white hot searing pain
that turns
and burns
purifies me,
makes me...
Gold.
Wrapped with Light
beyond thought,
when I have fought
and fight you
every time

until
I find
my strength:
surrender.
The ultimate
control?
Gifting it
to you,
to *you.*
You become
my Priest,
in that moment.
obsidian blade
in hand—
you want
Blood—
you
cannibalize
my heart,
my heart,
my
beating heart
trapped in your
fist.

I transubstantiate,
Sacred,
lost in
Sun
rising over edge
of
ancient mound,
you absolve
and
dissolve
me
till
my Wings burn,

and
I fall.

You
catch me,
dance
me.
Circle of sheets,
a bed
we cannot
Make Love in,
both too fucked up
in a fucked up
world,
so we fuck
and that has got
to be good enough
to make rain,
ensure harvest,
cure the sick,
and save
us all.

Putting Down Her Bundle

I have no time for weaklings subject to the whims of wild woman
    medicine,
those distracted by the foot-loose and fancy free.
Grown women carry burdens and need feet stronger than those of
    men.

I have no patience for fools putting hurt girls on pedestals,
expecting them to conduct themselves as queens.
I have no time for weaklings subject to the whims of wild woman
    medicine.

Blind worship is a prison, not a castle for the feminine.
A swift running prisoner makes her get-away clean.
Grown women carry burdens and need feet stronger than those of
    men.

Women warriors in life's battles need hearts that are garrisons.
Wise men look past those who pout and preen.
I have no time for weaklings subject to the whims of wild woman
    medicine.

Men who are veterans see the impediment
of a woman not grounded, pretty, but weak.
Grown women carry burdens and need feet stronger than those of
    men.

So don't be confused by the bait of estrogen.
Bright baubles can lead to traps unforeseen.
I have no time for weaklings subject to the whims of wild woman
    medicine.
Grown women carry burdens and need feet stronger than those of
    men.

Long Woman

You can't cross me—
My waters are too deep for you to ford,
too dangerous for you to ferry.

Like my mother, the Mississippi,
I writhe through red clay banks.
Drowned and wailing shades haunt my damp, green, caned and
willowed shores,
veiled in blackest night,
as I glide past,
silver serpent
painted with gold moon
and crystal stars.
Through morning mists I whisper new stories in ancient tongues
flowing to fertile deltas, cat-tailed marsh land,
warm, salty, dark Gulf undertow birthing hurricane squalls.

You can't cross me—
My waters are too deep for you to ford,
too dangerous for you to ferry.

The gator and gar
glide in my blood stream,
always looking for a next meal,
always ready to bite, to fight.
a coy grin framing flesh-ripping dinosaur teeth.
A forty-year-old blue cat
lies deep in my belly
turning charnel and shad
into thick steaks for my guests.
Pottery shard, bone fragment, stone disk, shell gorget
sift up from my vermillion silt.

You can't cross me—
My waters are too deep for you to ford,

too dangerous for you to ferry.

In my heart, there are hidden sinkholes,
holding remembered reflection, strange fruit swaying from thick,
gnarled oak branches above,
haunted by the ghosts of Confederate soldiers
and brown, wrinkled grandmas in heavy skirts whose calloused
feet drag circles in the mud.
There are immovable boulders,
refuge for horned and feathered Ukten
that defy potent medicine men and
burst master-engineered dams of precise masonry
like cottonmouths who skim my shallows,
guts distended with a meal of new hatchling,
break the surface unhindered.

You can't cross me—
My waters are too deep for you to ford,
too dangerous for you to ferry,
too deep for you to ford,
too dangerous for you to ferry.

IV. Mi Vida Comanchería

"Like a storybook ending I'm lost in your charms
And I could waltz across Texas with you..."
from "Waltz Across Texas," *Ernest Tubb's Greatest Hits*
recorded by Ernest Tubb, 1965
written by his cousin Quanah Talmadge Tubb

Ghost Haikus of Comanchería

Infant suckles breast.
Deer, Oreja de Raton.
Comanche Moon rises.

Quanah Parker's sage,
growing at the old home place,
cura, los celos.

Star House vacant, grey,
doors and windows left ajar.
Soft wind croons story.

Nopales, Hogplum,
Palo Blanco, Turkey Pear,
Mesquite and Weissach.

Rolling Pony's wives,
thrown away by the agent,
scattered across Plains.

Above the tipi,
the voices of Kakus sing
shrill in the moonlight.

Tasiwóo grazing
on starshine bathed blue bonnets.
Sage scent braces clear night.

Courtship

If you want to impress me,
wave your hand clockwise
above the fire pit,
peel back winter
with a thirty day
planetary spin,
steal me away
to Tejas
on a swift painted pony,
roll me in fields of bluebonnets,
paintbrushes,
and pink primroses,
fold up a quilt of
earth and flowers
to bed me a home
north of Red River,
snuggled in foothills
of the Wichitas,
in a clearing
in deep woods of Lake Ten Killer,
up in hills around Tulsa,
or down on the Muddy Boggy,
anywhere in Okla Humma that the roots can hold
and not get upturned
by the twisters
of life
or frozen out by its snows
and ice storms.

Pull a 1967
Arcadian Blue Mustang coupe
out of your back pocket,
drive circles
over plains,
through rivers and forests,

over mountains,
under oceans,
until you can
feed me cold,
sweet dewberries
'neath willows
while I call up catfish
from dark bottoms
for our supper.

When you whisper
to me,
do it in your language,
the tongue your grandpas wooed
your grandmas in.
Endearments in English
have grown stale
and dead to me
as corrupt human prayers
surely are to
God.

Hold me, Sweetheart,
safely in your arms.
Let me be the one you call "Honey," hey-yah.
Make here Home, if you really love me, Sugarpie.
Yeh yo hey-yah, yeh yo hi yah.
Hey-yah, hey-yah, ho…

Comanche Captive Love Poem#1

Tenahpu Penateka,
you taste like ocean water black dirt,
mesquite, *weissach,*
and Peyote.
You taste of cedar,
ancient, scattered, white seashell shards,
hot, hard Texas winds
of the Llano country,
Wichita Mountain breezes
at Medicine Bluffs.
You taste like the Heart of Jesus,
healing and redemption,
midnight water,
fireplace smoke,
and sage,
like dewdrops on my face, gazing up at the Morning Star.
You taste like Sunrise, Tabe Eka, promise of new beginning.

Comanche Captive Love Poem#2

The histories between us
are long and complex,
winding and drifting,
full of wars and treaties,
Numumu warriors, Texas Rangers,
San Antone Council House, Matilda Lockhart,
the German immigrant
and Chahta ancestors betwixt us.

We dance, feast, make love, negotiate,
battle again.
We eat each other's hearts
feed each other's spirits
please each other's bodies
tease and unease each other's minds
all at blinding frequency
in the space
outside time,
outside histories.

____
Our tears sweat blood bile
carve canyons
through mountains
trails
gaps
passages
we whisper
and writhe through
just for a chance
to touch each other
a handful of tangibility
to cling to.
I flounder without you
drown with you
in tides of other narratives,

remake this story,
swim
in the primeval ooze
the unseverable tangents
that connect us
as we flail
against
and
apart from
one another.

In this telling,
you walked
into and of me,
helped me bury my remains
in Mountains,
be reborn
and redeemed,
captured
and
set free in the bindings
of our story.

Comanche Captive Love Poem#3

I love what you become
when you do what you do to me,
metaphysical twists and turns
of serendipitous reality,
journeys in and out
of distinct physicality,
place beyond
darks and lights of you and me
where we just
    BE

____

Kamakuna
sumunahapu.
Nuhu puʔe?
Puha Hubiya.
Naʔnookatu,
numaʔai numunakatu
ma tukitu.
Tukanitu,
Tabeni...
Yunumitu.

____

Loved One,
become one.
Our path?
Medicine Songs.
Traveling together,
live with me
put in place.
Night,
Day...
live in a good way.

Comanche Captive Love Poem#4

Let me braid
and rebraid you,
work between sinew,
blood and bone,
taming taut muscle
and wild hair
under my flying fingers
into undulating patterns—
Snake medicine.
Sneak up puha.

——————————————————

Plains Sign Language for "marriage":

A grand pas de deux
of digits,
an entrechat,
notably missing
solo acts—
the parallel play of modern romance—
index fingers
briefly dancing
an introduction—
devant, derrière,
devant, derrière—
swing-stepping a half moon path,
coming together
in conclusion.

This isn't trade,
nor alliance,
rather conjugated confederation.

——————————————————

I bring my blanket,

my pipe and tobacco,
my books, plume and ink, papers,
my cache of corn.
Numu Tekwapu is a foreign language,
but I am an old traveler
and know
to bargain and jostle
for position.

____

Notsa? Kaaru.
I'll make kills
and take scalps for you,
be your Sweetheart Warrior
old style,
packing dry meat,
parched corn,
water bladders,
and a sharp knife.

Knock your enemies from their mounts—*wu tu kwai*—
Always Riding a Horse,
Wu yak aru,
I'll follow you,
translate, transform myself,
change my name.

Epilogue

"Girl I want to take you home...
Run wild horses, run..."
from "Run Wild Horses," *Vaquero,*
recorded by Aaron Watson, 2017

Texas... to Get Horses

"We went to Texas to get horses.
Your women followed us home."
Comanche men laugh, teasing the Mexicans.
All the Nums had captive grandmas.

"Your women followed us home."
Green eyes haunt hearts, stir blood memory.
All the Nums had captive grandmas.
My *tenapu's tsoo* was Guadalupe.

Green eyes haunt hearts, stir blood memory.
Nu naranapuu u, mis ojos verdes, nu pui, captured him.
My *tenapu's tsoo* was Guadalupe.
Nací en Tejas, I'm the best kind of captive there is.

Nu naranapuu u, mis ojos verdes, nu pui, captured him.
My buttermilk pie, chicken fried steak, guacamole,
and German noodles tethered him to me with silken bonds.
Nací en Tejas, I'm the best kind of captive there is.
I'm holding out on fried chicken until I get a ring.

My buttermilk pie, chicken fried steak, guacamole, and German
noodles tethered him to me with silken bonds.
Still, I'll tell you I'm his captive, *ihka kwuhupu.*
I'm holding out on fried chicken until I get a ring.
Na Numu naitu. I'm a quick study, Papi.

Still, I'll tell you I'm his captive, *ihka kwuhupu.*
I'm sassy and work harder than a hundred men.
Na Numu naitu. Im a quick study, Papi.
"We went to Texas to get horses."

*tenapu's tsoo-man's paternal grandmother
*Nu naranapuu u, mis ojos verdes, nu pui-my husband
("that's MY man"), my green eyes, my eyes
*Nací en Tejas—I was born in Texas
*ihka kwuhupu—wife ("well-assimilated captive")
*Na Numu naitu——to live as Comanche

Kimberly G. Wieser: Kimberly G. Wieser (formerly Roppolo) is a sixth-generation Texan of mixedblood ancestry who resides in Norman, Oklahoma, with her partner and cover artist Rance Weryackwe. She is an Associate Professor of English and affiliated faculty of Native American and Environmental Studies at the University of Oklahoma. Kimberly is a widely published creative and academic author whose work has appeared in *Sentence*, *Yellow Medicine Review*, *Great Plains Quarterly*, *Studies in American Indian Literatures*, *The American Indian Quarterly*, *Paradoxa* and many others. Her book, *Back to the Blanket: Recovered Rhetorics and Literacies in Native American Studies* (2017), based her manuscript that won the 2004 NWCA First Book Award for Prose, was published by University of Oklahoma Press. She is a co-author of *Reasoning Together: The Native Critics Collective*. Kimberly is an actress on AMC's *The Son* and in the short film *Thistle Creek*, of which she is also a producer and co-writer. Kimberly is a mom and a very, very young grandma.

Juanita Pahdopony: (Comanche Nation) is a renowned Comanche educator, poet and artist. She holds an A.A., B.A. and M.Ed. in art education. She has taught at Elgin Public Schools, Oklahoma City University, University of Science and Arts of Oklahoma, Cameron University, and Comanche Nation College. Pahdopony was Technical Advisor and consultant for Season 1 and 2 of AMC's *The Son* (summer 2016 through 2018). She was awarded the Roma Cliff Montgomery, 2018 Citizen of the Humanities, February 23, 2018, for the City of Lawton and the Lawton Arts & Humanities Council. She serves as a Board Member of Returning the Gift, Norman, Oklahoma (July 2016 to Present). Her poetry collection will be published with That Painted Horse Press in 2019.

Rance Weryackwe: (Comanche Nation) is an artist, actor on AMC's *The Son*, one of the producers of the short film *Thistle Creek*, and the author of "Savages Settlers, and Slaves: Red, White, and Black" (NativeNewsOnline). Most recently, he acted in a film for The Falls of the Ohio State Park Interpretive Center that will be part a permanent installation portraying 17,000 years of Indigenous American history in the area. An alumnus of The University of Oklahoma's Native American Studies Department (B.A. 2013; M.A. 2018), Rance lives in in Norman, Oklahoma, with his partner Kimberly and their daughters, Marley and Nia.

www.ingramcontent.com/pod-product-compliance
Lightning Source LLC
Chambersburg PA
CBHW031030190726
48286CB00003BA/1096